Pocket *Guide*
to
American Cooking
in
England

A guide for buying
American ingredients
in British supermarkets

Delora Jones

GLENCOE HOUSE PUBLICATIONS
BURTON UPON TRENT

Author's note:
Although this booklet is titled *The Pocketbook Guide to American Cooking in England*, I think you will find many of its entries apply to other parts of the British Isles as well. I used 'England' in the title rather than 'Britain' because that is where I live and that is the market I know (and the one the book is based on). Scotland, Wales, and Ireland have their own foods and markets and titling the book 'in Britain' would have ignored this fact. However, I have pointed out regional or national differences in food names or preparations whenever I've been aware of them.

First published 1998 by Glencoe House Publications
PO Box 5149, Burton upon Trent, Staffordshire DE14 3WZ
England

British Library Cataloguing in Publication Data
A catalogue record for this book is available from the British Library.

ISBN 0-9533557-1-3

Cover design by Visual Communication, Burton upon Trent
Book design by Delora Jones

Printed in Great Britain by John Mackie, Burton upon Trent

TABLE OF CONTENTS

INTRODUCTION

It shouldn't have surprised me, after all, I *was* in a foreign country, but it did surprise me. Grocery shopping for the first time in England took twice as long as it should have, and why? Because English food is not the same as American food. Things here are stocked differently, packaged differently, and called differently, and the issue is muddied by the fact that our two languages sometimes call different things by the same name (e.g., cider). It's true the US was founded by the British, but that was over 200 years ago and the food they ate then was, for the most part, different from what either of us eats now.

This pocketbook is designed to be consulted while grocery shopping for American ingredients[1] here, to help cut out wasted searches (like for corn syrup) and to steer you more quickly to the correct item.

In the *Foodnames* section, I've translated the names of food items from American to English, and said where to find these foods (or suitable substitutes). Also included are individual meat sections and diagrams, to help you select an appropriate British cut when an American cut of meat is called for.

The *Measurements* section contains the charts and conversion tables I found most helpful when cooking and buying food here.

Once you've got your bearings (food-wise, that is), I suggest you pick up a book on English cuisine (e.g., Jane Grigson's *English Food*). Their fine cuisine is a secret many of the natives don't even know.

---

[1]By 'American ingredients', I mean any ingredient whose American name is different from the British, e.g., 'eggplant' rather than *aubergine*.

FOOD NAMES

This section is essentially an A-Z of American foods, ingredients, and related items. The American name appears on the left and the English translation (or rough equivalent) appears in italics on the right. If you know the English name but not the American name, then check the Index.

Almonds, sliced	*Flaked almonds*
Anchovy paste	*Anchovy essence*
Angel hair pasta	*Vermicelli* (wheat-based)
Apples, candied	*Toffee apples*
Apples, McIntosh	*Empire apples* are similar.
Arugula	*Rocket* or *roquette*
Bacon	*Rindless unsmoked streaky bacon* is similar to American bacon. *Bacon rashers* are slices of bacon.
Bacon, Canadian	Similar to a *gammon steak*.
Bag, garbage	*Bin liner*
Bag, plastic grocery	*Carrier* or *carrier bag*
Baking powder	Although American baking powder is double-acting and British baking powder is single-acting, don't double the amount -- leave it as is and only adjust if necessary.
Baking soda	*Bicarbonate of soda* (sold in small round plastic containers)

Barley	*Pearl barley*
Beans, bush	*Dwarf beans*
Beans, fava	*Broad beans*
Beans, garbanzo	*Chick peas*
Beans, lima	Use *butter beans* in recipes calling for lima beans.
Beans, navy (or pea or Boston)	These are all names for *haricot beans*.
Beans, pole	*Climbing* or *runner beans*
Beans, string (also green or snap beans)	*Round beans*, *French beans* or *green beans* *French beans* are immature green beans so they're a bit thinner than the regular ones.
Beans, yellow wax	Not currently available (though the seeds *sometimes* are).
Beef cuts	See page 31.
Beef jerky	Beef jerky is available from Partridges, Harrods, and from Susmans (see *Addresses*, p.80).
Beer	For an American-style beer, ask for a *lager* (*beer* usually means *bitter,* the well-hopped English beer).
Beets	*Beetroot*
Biscuit	*Scone* (not a sweet scone)
Biscuit cutter	*Pastry cutter*

Blueberries	Blueberries are difficult to find here, but you can pick your own at James Trehane & Sons (Dorset) and Essington Fruit Farm (Wolverhampton). See *Addresses*, p.80.
Bologna	*Polony*
Bouillon cubes	*Stock cubes* or *stock granules*
Bread, Italian	This is not normally available here (at least, not in the Midlands).
Bread rolls	*Baps*, *plain tea cakes* or *cobs*.
Broccoli	*Broccoli* or *calabrese*.
Broil	*Grill*
Broiler	*Grill* *Grills* are usually situated above the main oven [often doubling as a second oven], or else above the *hob* (stovetop, US), at about eye-level.
Broiler (chicken)	*Spring chicken*
Broth, chicken	Canned chicken broth is only sold in speciality food shops.
Buns, sweet	*Tea cakes*
Burner	Gas burners are called gas burners but electric burners are called *rings*.
Butter, drawn	*Clarified butter*
Butter, sweet	*Unsalted butter*

Butter, whipped	Use *spreadable butter*
Butterfly shrimp	*Prawn cutlet*
Buttermilk	As of this writing, Sainsburys stock Raines' Live Cultured Buttermilk (near the yogurt). If you can't find any, you may use yogurt instead in most recipes.
Cabbage, Chinese	*Chinese leaf* or *leaf cabbage*
Cabbage, green	*White cabbage* or *green cabbage*
Cake	*Cake* or *gâteau*
Cake, angel food	*Angel cake*
Cake batter	*Cake mixture*
Cake, pound	Similar to *Madeira cake*
Cake, sheet	Technically speaking, a sheet cake is a single-layer cake baked in a 24" x 18" x 1" (*60cm* x *45cm* x *2.5cm*) pan; a half-sheet cake is one baked in an 18" x 12" x 1" pan (*45cm* x *30cm* x *2.5cm*). However, in the US the term "sheet cake" has come to mean any single-layer rectangular cake.
Cake pan, bundt	You may substitute using a Kugelhopf tin.
Cake pan, rectangular (for sheet cakes)	The typical size for rectangular cake pans is 13" x 9" x 2" (*33 x 23 x 5cm*).

Cake pan, round (for layer cakes)	*Round tin* or *sandwich tin*
Cake pan, spring-form	*Spring-clip tin*
Cake pan, tube	You may substitute using a Kugelhopf tin.
Calorie	*Kcal* British food labels list *Kj* (*Kilojoules*) and *Kcal* (*Kilocalories*). If you're counting calories, it's the *Kcal* amounts you need to add up.
Can	*Tin* or *can*
Can opener	*Tin opener*
Candied (e.g. candied ginger)	*Crystallized*
Candy	*Sweets* (or *chocolates*, if they're chocolate).
Candy bars	*Chocolate bars*
Candy, cotton	*Candy floss*
Candy, hard	*Boiled sweets*
Candy shots or non pareils	*Hundreds and thousands*
Candy sprinkles or jimmies	*Non pareils* or *vermicelli*
Canning jars	*Bottling* or *preserving jars*
Celery root	*Celeriac*

Cereals, breakfast	Sugar Pops are called *Sugar Puffs*; Coco Puffs are called *Coco Pops*; and Raisin Squares are called *Raisin Splitz*. Suffice it to say you'll have to look carefully when buying breakfast cereal in England.
Cheese, American	'Singles' Processed Cheese or Kraft 'Singles' (cheese food)
Cheese, colby	Substitute using a mild cheddar.
Cheese, cream	*Soft cheese* or *cream cheese* or *Philadelphia*
Cheese, farmer	See *Cheese, pot* this section.
Cheese, Monterey Jack	Substitute using a mild cheddar.
Cheese, Muenster	Substitute using a mild cheddar. NB: American Muenster cheese is very different from French Munster or German Münster and should not be confused with them.
Cheese, pot	This is sold in some speciality shops and Jewish delis. If you can't find it, use ricotta, or the drier Indian cheese, paneer (or farmer cheese, if available).
Cheese, ricotta	This is now sold in many supermarkets here but if you can't find it, use paneer (from an *Asian* shop), or cottage cheese (but first wrap it in

	cheesecloth [*muslin*] and hang it to drain).
Cheese, sharp	*Mature cheese*
Cheese, Swiss	use *Gruyère*
Cheese Whiz	*Cheese Spread* is similar.
Cheesecloth	*Muslin* or *butter muslin* (sold in fabric shops)
Cherries, candied	*Glacé cherries*
Cherries, maraschino	*Cocktail cherries (with maraschino flavouring)*
Chicken livers	Chicken livers are available from poulterers; kosher butchers; and sometimes frozen, in tubs, from the supermarket.
Chicken liver, chopped	You may use *chicken liver paté* as a substitute.
Chicken quarter or portion	*Chicken joint*
Chicory	*Endive* (curly-leaved)
Chiles, jalapeño	Jars of pickled jalapeños are sold in some supermarkets.
Chinese parsley	*Coriander leaves*
Chitterlings	Chitterlings in the US are cut up squares of pig's stomach and intestines; here *chitterlings* refer to sausages made from bits of intestine (usually pig's).

Chocolate, dark	*Plain chocolate*
Chocolate, semi-sweet baking	*Plain chocolate* or *bittersweet chocolate*
Chocolate, unsweetened baking	*Bitter chocolate*

Bitter chocolate is usually sold only in speciality shops. To substitute, use 3 tablespoons cocoa powder and 1 tablespoon butter, for each ounce of unsweetened chocolate.

Cider, apple	Non-alcoholic sweet apple cider is not widely available here but you can find apple juices made from crushed apples and tasting very similar to sweet cider.
Cider, hard	*Cider*

English alcoholic cider (called simply *cider*) is available anywhere that beer and wine are sold. Most *Cider* is carbonated and clear[2] (unlike the brownish and sometimes cloudy 'hard cider' sold in the US).

Cilantro[3]	*Coriander leaves*
Citrons	*Mixed peel* or *candied peel*
Clams	Categories of American clam include: Pacific hard-shell

---

[2] To be classed a cider, the alcohol content must be between 1.2 and 8.4%.

[3] Cilantro is the Spanish word for coriander leaves.

(1-2" [*2.5-5cm*]);
Atlantic hard-shell (1½"-4½"
[*4-11cm*]); and Atlantic soft-
shell (up to 2" [*5cm*]).
Clams have only recently been
introduced to a few areas in
Britain, so if you cannot find
clams locally, you may
substitute using cockles or
oysters for raw clams on the
half-shell recipes; cockles or
mussels for steamed clam
recipes; and mussels for fried
clam recipes.

Clam chowder, Manhattan	This is not currently sold in supermarkets here.
Clam chowder, New England	Although this chowder is not currently sold in English supermarkets, other milk-based fish chowders are.
Club soda	*Sparkling water* or *fizzy water*
Coconut, dried shredded	*Desiccated coconut*
Collard greens	Use kale or spring greens (e.g., beet, kohlrabi).
Cookie	*Biscuit* (though American-style cookies are labelled *cookies*)
Cookie cutter	*Pastry cutter* or *cookie cutter*
Cookie sheet	*Baking tray* or *baking sheet*
Cool Whip	Use a whipped cream topping.

Coriander leaves	You can get lovely large bunches from *Asian* shops or overpriced, bijou packets from most supermarkets.
Corn	*Sweetcorn* or *maize* In Britain, the word *corn* refers to a particular grain and, depending on where you are, that grain differs -- in England, *corn* means wheat; in Scotland, *corn* means oats.
Corn chips	These are not currently sold in supermarkets here, though tortilla chips are.
Corn, creamed	*Creamed* or *cream-style corn* is sometimes available in British supermarkets.
Corn syrup	Corn syrup is available only from specialty food shops. To substitute for dark corn syrup, mix 1 part *treacle* with 3 parts *glucose syrup* (and decrease the other sugars called for in the recipe by about half).[4] To substitute for light corn syrup, use *liquid glucose* or *glucose syrup*, but again, lessen the other sugars or syrups in the recipe. You may need to add a spoon or so of just-boiled water to get it the right consistency

---

[4] The sweetness of 1 cup of corn syrup is equal to that of ½ cup of sugar.

(*glucose syrup* is very viscous).
Boots sell it (from behind the counter), and other chemists and health food shops also sell it. (*Maize malt syrup* is <u>not</u> corn syrup.)

Corned beef (fresh only)	*Salt beef* or *cooked brisket* Here, *corned beef* refers to just tinned corned beef.
Cornmeal	*Polenta* (*coarse*), *maize meal* or *cornmeal*
Cornstarch	*Cornflour*
Crackers	*Savoury biscuits*
Cracker crumbs	Use crushed, savoury biscuits.
Cracklin' or crackling	In Britain, *cracklings* refer only to the crisp roasted skin of a pig (not to pig skin *or* chicken skin, as in the US).
Cranberries	Fresh cranberries are available from late November until just after Christmas.
Crawfish or crayfish	*Crayfish*
Cream Charts	See page 66.
Cream, heavy	use *Whipping cream*
Cream, light or coffee cream	use *Single cream*
Cream, sour	*Soured cream* or *sour cream* Alternatively, stir a drop or so of lemon juice or vinegar into single cream.

Cream, whipping	Use *whipping cream* (Alternatively, mix equal parts *single* and *double cream.*)
Cream of wheat	Cream of wheat is available in some specialty food shops.
Creamer	*Milk jug* or *creamer*
Crêpe	*Pancake* or *crêpe*
Crisco	See *Shortening* entry.
Crumbs, Graham cracker	Substitute using crushed digestive biscuits.
Crumbs, Italian bread	Use seasoned, dried bread crumbs, or season your own: to each cup of crumbs, add 3 Tbl. Parmesan; ¼ tsp. basil; and a ½ tsp. ea. of chives and oregano.
Cucumber	English cucumbers are the long 'hot house' variety so use only a 7" piece when a whole cuke is called for in an American recipe.
Cupcakes	*Fairy cakes*
Cymling (squash)	*Custard squash*
Dessert	*Afters* or *sweet* or *pudding*
Dinner (evening meal)	*Tea* or *dinner* *Dinner*, in England, means the main meal of the day whether served at night or mid-day.
Dish detergent	*Washing up liquid*

Dressing, French	*French dressing* or *vinaigrette* The orange-coloured, slightly viscous French dressing is not sold here, but the clear vinaigrette French dressing is.
Dressing, Russian	Though Russian dressing is not sold in supermarkets here, Thousand Island dressing is.
Dressing, salad	*Salad cream* The mayonnaise-like dressing that's called 'salad dressing' in the US is similar to *salad cream*.
Dressing, turkey	*Stuffing*
Dutch oven	*Flameproof casserole* or *iron camp oven*
Egg beater	*Rotary whisk* or *egg beater*
Eggplant	*Aubergine*
Egg roll	*Spring roll*
Eggs, white-shelled	White-shelled hen's eggs are not available here.
Electric beater or electric mixer	*Electric whisk* or *hand mixer*
Endive (or Belgian endive)	*Chicory* or *Brussels chicory*; also *Belgian* or *French endive*; or *witloof* (white leaf).
Escarole	*Batavia*, *batavia endive* or *escarole* (available from some speciality food shops)

Extract (e.g., vanilla extract)	*Essence* (e.g., *essence of vanilla*)
Fast food	*Take-away foods*
Faucet	*Tap*
Fettucine	*Vermicelli*
Filbert	use *cob nuts* or *hazelnuts*
Fish sticks	*Fish fingers*
Flan	*Créme caramel*
Flounder	Substitute using *plaice*
Flour, all purpose	*Plain flour*
Flour, bread or hard-wheat	*Strong flour*
Flour, cake	*Soft* or *softgrain flour* or *cake flour* (also known as *weak flour* and *household flour*)
Flour, self-rising	*Self-raising flour*
Flour, wholewheat	use *wholemeal flour*
Flowerets	*Florets*
French fries	*Chips*
Frosting	*Icing* and *soft icing* Blocks of *cake covering* (which you melt down for icing), are also sold here but the ones I've tried were disappointing.
Fruitcake	*Rich fruitcake* or *Christmas cake* Here, *fruitcake* is a moist

yellow cake laced with currants and cherries.

Fruit pitter	*Fruit stoner*
Garlic press	*Garlic crusher*
Gefilte fish	This is available from Jewish delis and some speciality shops.
Ginger ale	Ginger ale and ginger beer are both commonly available here.
Ginger root	*Root ginger*, also *ginger root*
Golden Fruit Raisin Biscuits	*Garibaldi*
Graham crackers and graham cracker crusts	These are not sold in English supermarkets so use *digestive biscuits* instead. For the crusts, combine 6 oz. (*170g*) crushed digestives with 2½ oz. (*70g*) melted butter. Press the mixture into the base and sides of a pie plate and chill for ½ an hour.
Granola	*Muesli* is very similar.
Green onions	*Spring onions* or *salad onions*
Grill (verb)	In the US, 'to grill' means to dry-cook something on a grill, such as a barbecue grill.
Grinder	*Baguette* (with a filling)
Grits	Grits are available from some speciality food shops.

Half & half	*Half cream* (or mix equal parts *single cream* and milk)
Hamburger	*Beefburger*
Hamburger buns	*Baps*, *plain tea cakes*, or *buns*
Hard sauce	*Rum butter* or *brandy butter*
Hazelnuts	Can use *cob nuts* instead.
Head cheese	*Brawn*
Hearts of palm	*Hearts of palm* or *palm hearts*
Hot dog tongs	*Serving tongs* or *kitchen tongs* or *tongs*
Ice cream	Use a farmhouse dairy ice cream or a supermarket's 'luxury' dairy ice cream when ice cream is called for in an American recipe.
Indian or Pakistani	*Asian* Here, Indian or Pakistani shops are usually called *Asian* shops.
Jawbreakers	*Gobstoppers*
Jello	*Jelly* Jelly here comes in a gelatinous block (not a powder).
Jelly, grape	Currently only available from speciality food shops.
Jelly roll	*Swiss roll*
Jelly roll pan	use a *Swiss roll tin*
Jewish food	For kosher shops, the main Jewish quarters are: Whitefield

in Manchester; Mosley in
Birmingham; and Golders
Green and Edgeware in
London.

Jicama	Can use white radish instead.
Junket rennet custard	*Rennet liquid* Junket rennet custard is not sold here but you can make junket from rennet liquid, which is available (or can be ordered) from chemists, speciality shops, and, currently, Safeway.
Kasha	*Roasted buckwheat* or *buckwheat groats* *Roasted buckwheat* is available from most health food shops.
Ketchup	*Tomato sauce* or *tomato ketchup*
Lamb cuts	See page 37.
Lasagne noodles	British lasagne has flat edges, is shorter than US lasagne, and 'requires no pre-cooking'.
Legumes	*Pulses*
Lemonade	*Homemade* or *fresh lemonade* Here, *lemonade* is a carbonated lemon-flavoured soda (also called *sparkling lemonade*).
Lettuce, Boston or butterhead	*Round lettuce* or *flat lettuce*
Lettuce, romaine	*Cos lettuce*

Liquor, hard	*Spirits*
Liverwurst	*Liver sausage* (or, *liver pâté*).
Lox	*Smoked salmon*
Manicotti	use *cannelloni*
Marshmallows	White and coloured marshmallows are often packaged together here, so check before buying.
Martini	In England, *martini* usually refers to vermouth alone.
Masa harina	Available only in specialty shops. Alternatively, use cornmeal (*coarse polenta*).
Matzo or matzo meal	Both are available from Jewish delis and butchers.
Measuring cup	*Measuring jug* or *glass*
Measuring spoons	British sets typically include ½ teaspoon; 1 teaspoon (*5 ml*); dessertspoon (*10 ml*); and tablespoon (*15 ml*). American sets usually have ¼ teaspoon instead of a dessertspoon.
Meat grinder	*Hand operated mincer*
Melon, honeydew	The honeydew sold here is the *large yellow honeydew*; I have not seen the pale-green skinned ones (like in the US) here.
Mimosa	*Buck's fizz*
Milk Chart	See page 64.

Milk, 1% (and 2%)	See *Milk, lowfat*
Milk, condensed	In England, condensed milk is milk which is pasteurized, evaporated milk is not; so here there's a separate product called *unsweetened condensed milk*
Milk, dry or powdered	*Dried milk, powdered milk,* or *dehydrated milk* To reconstitute, add 2 oz. dried milk to every 20 oz. of water.
Milk, evaporated	American evaporated whole milk must contain at least 7.9% milkfat; in Britain, it must contain at least 9% fat.
Milk, lowfat	*Semi-skimmed milk,* also *half-fat milk*
Milk, skim and nonfat	*Skimmed milk*
Milk, ultrapasteurized	*UHT milk* or *long life milk*
Milk, whole	*Whole milk,* also *full cream milk* By definition *full cream milk* refers to Channel Islands milk (with its higher milkfat content), but now it's loosely used to refer to any whole milk.
Miracle Whip	use *salad cream*
Mirin	Mirin is available in the larger Oriental stores; in select Sainsburys; and some Asian

	shops. Alternatively, substitute using $2/3$ cup ($5^1/3$ oz.) dry sherry and $1/3$ cup ($2^1/2$ oz.) sugar to equal one cup of mirin.
Molasses	Molasses is available in some speciality shops and health food shops, but rarely in supermarkets. Alternatively, substitute using equal parts of golden syrup and treacle.
Muffins	*American muffins*
Muffins, English	*Muffins*
Muffin pan or muffin tin	Muffin tins are available in most cookery shops.
Napkins, table	*Serviettes*
Noodles, broad or wide	These are only available in speciality food shops.
Noodles, egg	*Tagliatelle*
Nuts	*Nuts* or *kernels*
Oil, corn	*Corn oil* or *maize oil*
Oil, peanut	*Groundnut oil* or *peanut oil*
Oil, salad	This is any oil suitable for dressing salads.
Okra	*Okra* or *ladies fingers*
Oleo (oleomargarine)	*Margarine*
Olives, ripe	*Black olives*
Orange juice	Orange juice is available in boxes, and in chilled cartons

from the supermarket; also in
pint bottles from your milkman.
Currently Sainsburys carry a
frozen concentrate, but I find
its taste somewhat bitter.

Organ meat	*Offal*
Oven mitts	*Oven gloves* or *oven mitts* Note: *double oven gloves* refer to a long rectangular piece of thick fabric, with pockets at each end (for your hands).
Oyster	Oysters sold in Britain include 'natives' (*Ostrea edulis*); Portuguese or 'Ports' (*Crassotrea angulata*); and the giant Pacific oyster or 'gigas' (*Crassotrea gigas*). You may eat 'Ports' and 'gigas' any time but only eat 'Natives' when there's an 'r' in the month.
Oyster cracker	These are not currently sold in supermarkets here.
Pan	*Tin* Bread pans are called *loaf tins*.
Pancake	Whereas American pancakes are thick; British pancakes are the same as crêpes (thin).
Pan-broil	Pan-broiling is cooking meat in a frying pan *without* added fat.
Pan-fry	*Fry* (as opposed to deep-fat frying)

Papaya	*Pawpaw* or *papaya*
Paper towels	*Kitchen towels* or *absorbent kitchen paper*
Partridge	*Quail* or *grouse* In northern US, partridge refers to *ruffed grouse*; in the south it means *quail*.
Pasta, Bows	*Farfalle*
Pasta, Shells	*Conchiglie*
Patty pan (cymling)	*Custard squash*
Peanut Butter Cups	These are sold in Woolworth's.
Pears, Bartlett	*Williams pears*
Peas, black-eyed	*Black-eyed beans* are available in many health food shops and some supermarkets.
Pepper shaker	*Pepper pot*
Peppers, bell (also green, sweet or globe)	*Capsicum peppers* or *sweet peppers*
Periwinkles	*Winkles*
Piccalilli	English *piccalilli* is closer to what Americans call mustard pickle or chow chow, than it is to American piccalilli.
Pickles, half-sour	These are available from Jewish delis and speciality food shops.
Pie dough	*Shortcrust pastry*

Pie plate	American pie plates usually have an 8 or 9" (*20-23 cm*) diameter and a narrow, flat rim; they're deeper (1-1½" [*2.5-4 cm*]) than British pie plates.
Pie shell or pie crust	*Pastry case*
Pit (e.g., cherry pit)	*Stone*
Plastic wrap	*Cling film*
Popcorn	Popcorn is often prepared 'sweet' here so be sure to check before buying. Otherwise, make your own: the kernels are sold in health food shops, and fruit & nut stalls.
Popsicles	*Ice lollies* *Ice lollies* sold in the UK often contain an artificial sweetener.
Pork cuts	See page 43.
Pot	*Pan* Here, *pan* refers to a stovetop cooking vessel while *pot* refers to a container for holding liquids or solids (e.g., like an American casserole dish.)
Potato, sweet	Supermarkets here have, in the past, carried both types of sweet potato (usually not at the same time) so check first before buying your other ingredients.
Potato chips	*Crisps* or *potato crisps*

Pretzel	Crisp pretzels are sold in some British supermarkets.
Prosciutto	use *Parma* or *Serrano ham*
Pumpernickel	Pumpernickel bread is available in some speciality shops and occasionally, supermarkets.
Pumpkin, canned	*Tinned pumpkin* is available in some speciality shops and, now and then, in supermarkets. Otherwise, buy them fresh in the autumn (if you can find them), and make your own puree.
Quiche	*Savoury flan* or *quiche*
Quiche pan	*Flan dish*
Raisins, black	*Raisins* sold here include seedless California ones and also, highly regarded muscatel varieties, which contain pips.
Raisins, golden or white	*Sultanas*
Roast (*n*)	*Joint* (as in 'a joint' [of beef])
Root beer	Root beer is only available in speciality food shops.
Rutabaga	*Swede* (or *turnip* in Scotland)
Rye bread	Rye bread has recently become available in many supermarkets.
Rye flour	This is sold in health food shops and some supermarkets.

Saccharin	In England, saccharin is often used as an inexpensive sugar substitute, so always read the list of ingredients to check.
Sage, dried or ground	*Rubbed sage*
Salt, kosher	Small containers of kosher salt are available from Jewish delis and some supermarkets.
Salt shaker	*Salt cellar* (or, less commonly, *salt shaker*)
Sandwich, chicken salad	In England, this means a sandwich made with chicken meat and salad ingredients (e.g., cress; cucumber; tomato).
Sarsaparilla	This is sold in markets in the north (e.g., Blackburn market). For an extract to make your own, see *Addresses* for Walsh's.
Sausage, bulk pork	*Sausage meat*
Scallions	*Spring onions* or *salad onions*
Scampi	*Scampi* or *Dublin Bay prawn*
Scotch	*Whisky* In England, *whisky* refers to scotch whisky.
Sell by date	*Display until date* (Note: products should be consumed before their *Best before end* or *BBE* date.)
Seltzer	*Fizzy water*, *sparkling water* or *carbonated water*

Sherbet	*Sorbet* is very similar to US sherbet. In England, *sherbet* often refers to a powdered candy (similar to Lik 'm Ade).
Shortening	Use *White sunflower vegetable fat*, *White Flora*, or *Trex* Packed in 500g boxes, you'll find these in the refrigerated section of the supermarket.
Shrimp	In England, *shrimp* and *prawns* (i.e., large shrimp) are often sold already cooked.
Shrimp, butterfly	*Prawn cutlet*
Skillet	*Frying pan* In England, *skillet* normally refers to a small, long-handled, metal pot (usually with legs).
Snow peas	*Mange tout* (i.e., eat all)
Soda or soda pop	*Soft drink* or *fizzy drink*
Sourdough bread	You can make this yourself by letting yeast ferment and then adding it to the flour, but it won't taste the same flavour as San Francisco's (which is made from a particular yeast strain).
Soy	*Soya* (except for the sauce which is called *soy sauce*)
Spatula (metal)	*Fish slice* or *lifter*
Spoon, slotted	*Straining spoon*

Sprouts	When an American recipe doesn't specify the type of sprouts, use a sprouted seed like *cress* or *salad cress*.
Squash, spaghetti	*Vegetable spaghetti*
Squash, summer	I've never seen yellow summer squash for sale here and, only occasionally, have I seen *yellow courgettes*, though I have seen their seeds. NB: *Squash* here is more commonly known as a fruit drink concentrate.
Stove	*Cooker* In England, *stove* usually refers to an old-style gas stove.
Stovetop	*Hob*
Strainer	*Metal sieve* or *strainer*
Submarine sandwich or hoagie or grinder	*Baguette* (This is both the name of the bread as well as the filled sandwich.)
Sugar, brown	For American recipes calling for dark brown sugar, use *rich dark soft sugar* or *dark brown muscovado*; for light brown sugar, use *light golden soft sugar* or *light brown muscovado*.
Sugar, confectioners or powdered	*Icing sugar*
Sugar, granulated	Use *granulated sugar* (but if using *caster sugar* in its place,

	adjust the amount called for as its crystal size is approximately half that of granulated).
Sugar, superfine	*Caster sugar*
Sugar, turbinado	*Demerara sugar*
Supper	*Tea* or *dinner* In England, *supper* refers to a light, late night (e.g., 9pm) meal.
Swiss chard	*Swiss chard* or *seakale beet* (or use baby beet greens)
Tacos	Taco shells are available in British supermarkets.
Taffy or toffee	*Toffee*
Take-out food	*Take-away food*
Tea, iced	The English do not drink iced tea though I did see cans of it at Safeway once (carbonated!).
Tomato paste	*Double concentrated tomato puree*
Tomato puree	Use Safeway's *Creamed tomatoes*. Alternatively, puree skinned tomatoes in a blender.
Tomato sauce	Use *Passata* or *salsina* (NB: tomato sauce should be slightly thinner than puree.)
Tortilla	You can now find tortillas in most British supermarkets.
Turnip, French	*White-fleshed swedes*

Vanilla bean	*Vanilla pod*
Variety meats	*Offal*
Veal cuts	See page 53.
Vegetables, raw	*Crudités*
Walnut, English	*Walnut* Though not the same as the American (or black) walnut, either may be used in recipes.
Wax paper	use *baking parchment* or *greaseproof paper*
Wheat	*Wheat* (in England, it's also called *corn* -- see Corn entry)
Wheat berries	*Wheat grains* (also *whole wheat grains*) or *wheat kernels*
Whisk	*Balloon whisk* or *whisk*
Whiskey	*American rye whiskey* (or simply *rye*) is difficult to find here but you can usually find Canadian rye whisky.
Wholewheat bread	*Wholemeal bread*
Yeast, active dry	*Dried* or *dried active yeast* These yeasts must be proofed.
Yeast, 'fast-action', 'quick-rise', or 'rapid-rise' dried	Use *'easybake'* or *'easy-blend'* *dried yeast* Do not proof these yeasts -- just add them to the dry ingredients.
Yogurt, unflavoured	*Natural yogurt*
Zucchini	*Courgettes*

NOTES

BEEF CUTS

I have listed below some popular American cuts of beef. You'll notice that the American cuts often do not have an exact British counterpart, so check the descriptions below for the section of cow the meat is from, and look for a similar British cut from that section. By the way, when the British name of the same [or roughly the same] section of cow is different from the American name, I've included both names (with the British name in italics). If still in doubt, ask the butcher for advice.

Châteaubriand	Steaks used for making Châteaubriand are cut on the diagonal from the thickest part of the tenderloin or *fillet of beef* and range in thickness from 2" - 3" (*5-7.5cm*).
Chuck cross rib, chuck rib, chuck roast, and chuck arm steak	'Chuck' cuts come from the chuck or chuck shoulder section of the cow. The same section in England is called *chuck* or *chuck blade*. In Scotland, *chuck* and *blade* combined are known as *shoulder*.
Club steak	See Top loin steak.
Corned beef brisket	*Salt beef*
Cubed steak	*Stewing steak*

BEEF CUTS, *cont.*

AMERICAN BEEF CUTS

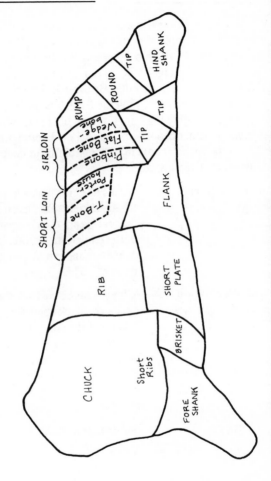

BEEF CUTS, *cont.*

BRITISH BEEF CUTS

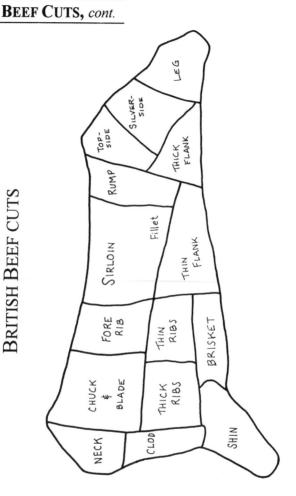

BEEF CUTS, *cont.*

Delmonico steak, rib eye steak, or Spencer steak	*Rib eye steak* These are 1" (*2.5cm*) boneless steaks cut from the eye of the rib roast.
Eye of rib roast	This is the cut traditionally used for English roast beef.
Filet mignon	*Filet mignon* or *filet mignon tournedos*
Fillet steaks	These cuts go by the same name in England as in the US.
Foreshank	*Shin*
Ground beef	*Minced beef* *Minced beef* is sold in a fine or coarse mince; fine mince is similar to American ground beef.
Hindshank	*Leg*
Loin tenderloin steak	*Fillet steak*
London broil or flank steak	London broil is an inexpensive and boneless cut from the flank section. (Also known as flank steak in the US but unrelated to British flank.)
Porterhouse steak	Also known as Porterhouse in England, these steaks are from the section here called *sirloin*.
Rib eye steaks	See Delmonico steak.

BEEF CUTS, *cont.*

Rib roast or prime rib	These cuts come from the rib (*forerib*) section.
Round steak or round roast	This is the same cut of meat as is used for the English cut called *rump steak*.
Sandwich steak	Use *very* thinly sliced steak from either the *topside* or *silverside* sections.
Shank	The foreshank is the *shin*; the hindshank is the *leg*.
Shell steak	See Top loin steak.
Short plate	In England, this lies at the *brisket* end of the *flank* or *thin flank* section.
Short ribs and chuck short ribs	In the US, short ribs are cut from the ribs between the rib and short plate sections while chuck short ribs are from the ribs between the chuck and brisket sections. Roasts for home use are often cut short and the resulting cut-off rib ends are the short ribs which are normally braised or marinated and barbecued.
Sirloin steak	Also known as *sirloin steak* in England.

Sirloin steak, boneless *Entrecôte*

BEEF CUTS, *cont.*

Spencer steak	See Delmonico steak.
Swiss steak	For Swiss steak, use a 1½" (*4 cm*) thick cut of meat from the *rump, topside, silverside,* or *chuck and blade* sections.
T-bone steak	This steak is from the section called *sirloin* in England.
Tenderloin of beef or fillet of beef	*Fillet of beef*
Tenderloin steak	*Fillet steak*
Top loin steaks (e.g., strip, shell, and club steaks)	When the top loin section of the cow is boned out, the fillet removed, and the remaining meat then cut into steaks, the result is top loin steaks.
Tournedos	Also known as *tournedos* in England.

LAMB CUTS

Many of the popular cuts of lamb in England are different from the popular US cuts, so when my description of an American cut does not include an equivalent British cut, tell your butcher the section of the animal the cut is from and see if he can suggest an alternate cut. As American and British butchers cut up a sheep somewhat differently, I've included illustrations showing the differences.

Note: In Scotland, a shoulder is cut as a larger joint, and includes part of the neck and the breast. This shoulder joint is then divided into 2 or 3 joints, which are often boned, stuffed, and rolled into roasts. Also, the Scottish leg of lamb (called *gigot*) includes the *chump* end of the loin. *Gigot* is usually divided into 3 sections: *chump*, *centre*, and *knuckle*.

Breast of lamb	In the US, it's often boned and trimmed of fat, then rolled and tied and sold as rolled breast or, if it's stuffed as well, sold as stuffed breast. In England, the cut called *rolled breast* is normally already stuffed.
Crown roast	This roast from the rib or rack (*best end of neck*) section, is constructed by tying together 2 racks of trimmed ribs (*2 trimmed best ends*), to form a crown. You'll need to allow a few days for your butcher to prepare one.

LAMB CUTS, *cont.*

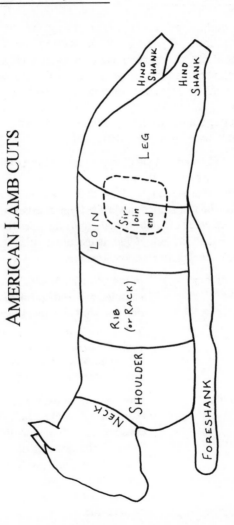

AMERICAN LAMB CUTS

LAMB CUTS, *cont.*

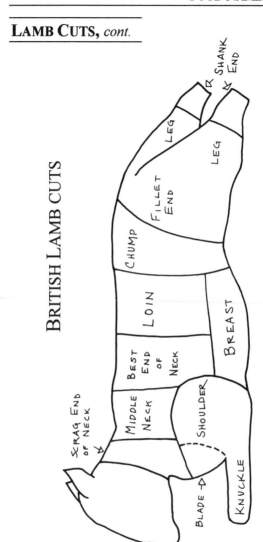

BRITISH LAMB CUTS

LAMB CUTS, *cont.*

Frenched leg of lamb	With this cut, an inch or so of the shank bone is exposed.
Frenched rib chops	*French lamb cutlets* These chops from the rib or rack (*best end of neck*) section of the sheep contain rib eye muscle and a rib bone, the end of which is trimmed of meat.
Lamb neck slices	Also known in the US as lamb shoulder neck slices; lamb neck; and lamb for stew, bone in. These round slices contain a cross section of the neck bone.
Lamb patties	Lamb patties (or lamburgers) are burgers made from lamb.
Lamb shank, lamb foreshank, or lamb trotter	This cut is the foreshank (or *knuckle*) end of the arm or front leg, and contains the round leg bone.
Leg chop	*Leg fillet*
Leg of lamb, whole or leg roast, sirloin on	This cut includes the sirloin section of the leg (with the hip bone) and the shank portion of the leg (with the round leg bone). In the US, this cut weighs between 4½ - 9 lbs. (here, it's from a younger sheep, so it's around 4 - 5½ lbs).

LAMB CUTS, *cont.*

Leg, shank half

The shank half (*knuckle end* or *shank end*) is the lower half of the hind leg and contains the round leg bone.

Leg, sirloin or butt end

Fillet of lamb
This is the sirloin end (*fillet end*) of the leg.

Loin chops

These are roughly equivalent to English loin chops.

Rib chops or rack lamb chops

Best end chops or *best end of neck cutlets (or chops)*
These chops are from the rib or rack (*best end of neck*) section of the sheep and contain rib eye muscle and a rib bone.

Rib roast, rack roast, or rib rack

The lamb rib roast is from the rib or rack (*best end of neck*) section of the sheep. It contains rib bones, backbone, and thick, meaty rib eye muscle. When the rib eye muscle is removed from the rack and sliced into thick steaks, these slices are known as medallions.

Riblets or breast riblets

Lamb riblets are long and narrow 1-1½" cuts from the breast section, containing the rib bone.

LAMB CUTS, *cont.*

Rolled loin roast	This is the loin roast but with the T-bone removed, and then rolled and tied.
Rolled shoulder	This shoulder cut is boned, rolled, and tied, and is suitable for roasting or braising.
Saddle	Also called *saddle* in England, this is the whole loin section, cut out in one saddle-shaped piece, and often with the kidneys tied in with it. Note: Your butcher will need a few days' notice to prepare one.
Saratoga chops	Saratoga chops are slices from the shoulder which are boned, rolled, and then skewered (to keep them from unrolling).
Shoulder arm chop, arm cut, or round bone chop	The lamb shoulder arm chop is cut from the shoulder and contains the round arm bone.
Shoulder blade chop or blade cut chops	This cut from the shoulder contains the blade bone.
Sirloin chops	These are roughly equivalent to English *chump chops* and come from the sirloin (*chump*) section.

PORK CUTS

In the US, we do not have a cut of meat called gammon, and without going into over much detail, suffice it to say that gammon is quite similar to ham (i.e., they are both a cured hind leg of a pig).

American pork cuts may differ somewhat from the English cuts so I have not always tried to give equivalents. Instead, I have listed the American name and described the cut, and said which section of the animal the cut is from. (Note: Though an English cut may have the same name as an American cut, the cuts themselves may be different.)

Bear in mind that although the BRITISH PORK CUTS diagram that follows is, for the most part, correct for England, there are regional differences, as well as differences between the way a Scottish and English pig is cut up. The *hand & spring* section (comprised of the lower shoulder [the hand], the jowl, knuckle, trotter, and first 3 or 4 bones of the belly) is, in northeast England, called *shoulder*, and in Scotland, called a *runner*. (Also, in Scotland, the *knuckle* is called a *hough*.) The *neck end* (i.e., the upper part of the shoulder consisting of the *spare rib* and *blade*) is, in northeast England, called a *chine* and in Scotland called *shoulder*. (Also, the Scottish *shoulder* is cut larger and may weigh as much as 20 lbs.) And, as in lamb, the leg of the animal is, in Scotland, called *gigot*.

Some common American cuts of pork follow.

PORK CUTS, *cont.*

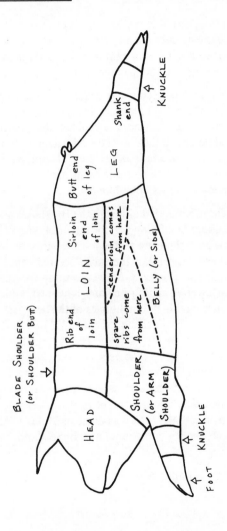

AMERICAN PORK CUTS

KNUCKLE

Shank end

LEG

Butt end of leg

Sirloin end of loin

tenderloin comes from here

BELLY (or Side)

LOIN

Rib end of loin

spare ribs come from here

BLADE SHOULDER (or SHOULDER BUTT)

HEAD

SHOULDER (or ARM SHOULDER)

KNUCKLE

FOOT

PORK CUTS, *cont.*

BRITISH PORK CUTS

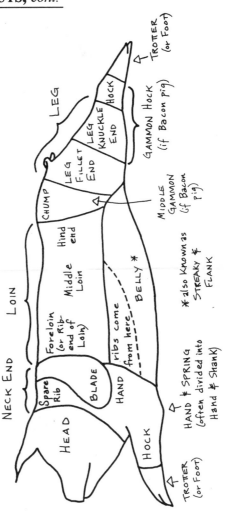

TROTTER (or Foot)

GAMMON HOCK (if Bacon pig)

HOCK

LEG KNUCKLE END

LEG FILLET END

CHUMP

LEG

Hind end

Middle Loin

Foreloin (or Rib-end of Loin)

LOIN

NECK END

Spare Rib

BLADE

HAND

ribs come from here

HEAD

HOCK

HAND & SPRING (often divided into HAND & SHANK)

TROTTER (or Foot)

MIDDLE GAMMON (if Bacon pig)

BELLY *

* also known as STREAKY & FLANK

PORK CUTS, *cont.*

Arm roast or shoulder arm roast	This cut from the lower portion of the shoulder (*hand and spring*) section has the shank removed and contains a small round bone.
Arm steak	This slightly oval steak is cut from the arm roast and contains a small round (arm) bone.
Back ribs	Back ribs are from the loin section near the shoulder blade and have very little meat on them.
Boston butt roast	See Shoulder blade roast.
Bulk pork sausage	*Sausage meat*
Butterfly chops	A butterfly chop is made from a boneless chop from the loin section. To make a butterfly chop, cut a boneless pork chop almost in half (so that it's half as thick as it was), and spread each side out flat so that its shape resembles a butterfly.
Country-style ribs	Country-style or country ribs are meaty ribs from the loin section and contain either rib bones or backbones.
Fatback	*Back fat* *Back fat* is fresh (as opposed to cured, salted, or smoked) and is

PORK CUTS, *cont.*

	sold for larding meat; for barding; and for lining molds for pâtés.
Fresh ham slice or center slice	This oval-shaped cut is from the hind leg of the animal and contains a small round bone and 4 separate muscles.
Head cheese	*Brawn*
Loin blade roast (also 5-rib roast, 7-rib roast, and rib end roast)	This roast is cut from the shoulder end of the loin section and contains a portion of the blade and rib bones.
Loin center rib roast or center cut pork roast	This roast is from the centre of the loin. It contains loin eye muscle and rib bones and is very dear.
Loin chops or loin end chops	Pork loin chops are from the loin section and contain loin and tenderloin muscles, usually with a T-shaped bone separating the muscles.
Loin rib chops, center cut pork chops, or rib chops	These chops are smaller and less choice than the chops known simply as loin chops. They are cut from the rib end of the loin and contain rib bone but no tenderloin.
Loin sirloin chops or sirloin pork chops	These are from the sirloin end (or *hind end*) of the loin and

PORK CUTS, *cont.*

	contain a bone. *Chump chops* would make a suitable substitute.
Loin sirloin cutlets	These are boneless tender slices cut from the sirloin end (or *hind end*) of the loin. *Noisettes* or *boneless chump chops* would make suitable substitutes.
Picnic	See Shoulder arm picnic.
Pig's feet	*Trotters*
Pork hocks	Pork hocks are cut from the 'picnic shoulder', which is from the shoulder (*hand and spring*) section. The hock is the 2-3" (*5-7.5cm*) piece that's removed from the end of the picnic shoulder when it is cut short. They are round, tapering, skin-covered pieces containing shank bones and some very edible meat.
Pork leg, whole or 'fresh' ham	This cut contains the hind leg bone.
Pork sausage	The minced pork used in American pork sausage is normally from the blade shoulder section. American pork sausage may or may not be smoked.

PORK CUTS, *cont.*

Rib crown roast	To get a rib crown roast, you fasten together two loin roasts in the shape of a crown.
Rolled Boston butt	See Shoulder blade roast, boneless.
Shoulder arm picnic or picnic	The picnic shoulder is from the shoulder (*hand and spring*) section and contains the forearm and shank.[5] It is cut deep into the shoulder, around and down to the front foot, in the shape of a small ham.
Shoulder blade roast, Boston butt, or pork butt	This roast is from the upper shoulder (*blade*) and contains a portion of the blade bone.
Shoulder blade roast, boneless	This roast (also known as boneless blade roast and rolled Boston butt) is the shoulder blade roast boned, rolled, and tied. (See Shoulder blade roast.)
Shoulder blade steak or blade steak	This steak is cut from the shoulder blade roast. (See Shoulder blade roast.)
Sirloin roast	A sirloin roast is a roast cut from the sirloin end (*hind end*) of the loin.

[5]The shank section is that nearest the knuckle.

PORK CUTS, *cont.*

Spareribs
Spare ribs
Not to be confused with the *spare rib joint* of an English pig -- that is near the head, and cuts from it are called *spare rib chops*; these spareribs are from the belly section and are long rib bones with a very thin covering of meat.

Tenderloin
Fillet
The tenderloin (or *fillet*) is the lean, tender muscle that lies beneath the backbone at the sirloin end (*hind end*) of the loin.

CURED CUTS:

Bacon
Rindless unsmoked streaky bacon and *Danish plain (or unsmoked) streaky rindless bacon*, are similar to American-style bacon. American bacon is saltier and yields more fat than English bacon, and whereas the sliced bacon sold in the US is rindless, *bacon rashers* (i.e., slices of bacon) sold here come with or without a rind so you may need to trim the rind.

PORK CUTS, *cont.*

CURED CUTS, *cont.*

Canadian bacon	A *gammon steak* would make a reasonable substitute.
Ham, country	Country hams are hams which are more heavily cured and smoked than the ready-to-eat hams sold in American supermarkets; also they are much tastier. Before boiling or baking, they must first be soaked.
Prosciutto	use *Parma ham* or *Spanish Serrano ham*
Salt pork	Salt pork is primarily fat, with some streaks of lean, and comes from the part of the pig known as the side pork or siding (below the loin and extending through the centre of the pig).
Smoked ham center slice	This cut comes either with the round arm bone or boneless, and ranges from ½"-2" thick.
Smoked ham rump portion (or butt half)	This cut is from the upper portion or butt half of the ham (minus several center slices).
Smoked ham shank portion	This piece is cut from the lower portion or shank half of

PORK CUTS, *cont.*

CURED CUTS, *cont.*

	the ham (minus several center slices), and is usually less expensive than the upper portion which is called the butt half.
Smoked pork shoulder picnic	A smoked picnic (also known as picnic ham and smoked callie) is essentially a ham made from the *front* leg of the pig rather than the back leg.
Smoked whole ham	This is cured and smoked whole pork leg and weighs anywhere from 12-14 pounds.

VEAL CUTS

American and British cuts of veal do not exactly correspond, so I've included in the descriptions of the cuts, which section of the animal the cut is from. On the following 2 pages are illustrations showing how a British butcher cuts up a veal carcass and also how an American butcher cuts one up. (If in doubt, describe the cut to your butcher.)

Some common American cuts of veal are listed below.

Arm roast	Arm roast is cut from the shoulder and contains the arm bone (a round bone) and usually part of the rib bones.
Arm steak	Arm steak is an oval-shaped steak cut from the shoulder and contains the arm bone and a rib bone.
Breast of veal	The lean cut is from the breast area under the rib section. It is a thin, flat cut containing the breast bone, lower ribs, and rib cartilage.
Breast riblets or veal riblets	These rectangular strips of meat are made by cutting between the ribs. They're from the breast section and contain rib bones.
Breast roast, boneless	This roast is the breast of veal boned, rolled, and tied.

VEAL CUTS, *cont.*

AMERICAN VEAL CUTS

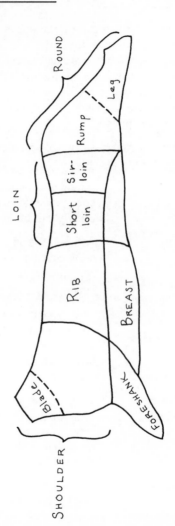

VEAL CUTS, *cont.*

BRITISH VEAL CUTS

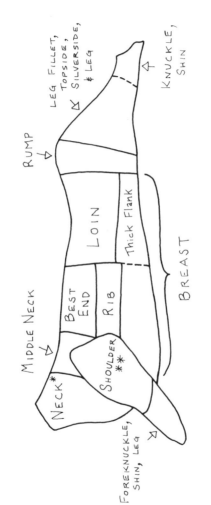

Leg Fillet, Topside, Silverside, & Leg

Knuckle, Shin

Rump

Loin

Thick Flank

Breast

Middle Neck

Best End

Rib

Neck*

Shoulder **

Foreknuckle, Shin, Leg

* also known as Scrag End.
** also known as Clod.

VEAL CUTS, *cont.*

Crown roast

A crown roast is cut from the rib section (the *best end* section in England). The tips of the rib bones are trimmed of fat and lean, and then fastened to form a crown.

Cube steak

Veal cube steak is a mechanically tenderised cut from the shoulder, loin, or round (*leg fillet*) sections.

Cutlets, veal

Escalopes or *fillets*
In the US, veal cutlets are thin, boneless slices from the leg section; in England, the cutlets come from the *best end* section and contain a bone (see Rib chop). American cutlets are usually ½-¾" (*12-19mm*) thick and are often pounded, especially in recipes calling for rolling or stuffing.

Leg rump roast

Veal leg rump roast (also known as veal rump roast or rump of veal) contains the leg bone and is from the rump section (or, in England, the *rump* and *leg fillet* sections).

Leg rump roast, boneless

Boneless leg rump roast (also known as rolled rump roast or rump of veal, boneless) is the leg rump roast with the leg

VEAL CUTS, *cont.*

	bone removed, and the roast rolled and tied. It comes from the rump section (or, in England, the *rump* and *leg fillet* sections).
Loin chops	Veal loin chops contain tenderloin and are similar to beef Porterhouse steaks in that they have a T-bone and a fair portion of lean meat.
Loin roast	Veal loin roast is cut from the loin section and contains the T-bone.
Ossi buchi or osso buco	*Osso buco* *Osso buco* calls for slices of veal shank, 1½" thick, with bone and marrow. Veal shank is cut from the foreshank or *foreknuckle* section.
Rack	*Best end* A rack is a roast of rib chops. The section it is from is called the rib section in the US and the *best end* section in England.
Rib chop	*Cutlets* A rib chop contains a rib bone and rib eye muscle (but not the tenderloin). The section it is

VEAL CUTS, *cont.*

	from is called the rib section in the US and the *best end* section in England.
Rib roast	*Best end* A rib roast has 2 or more ribs and includes the rib eye muscle, featherbones and part of the chine bone (i.e., the thick part where the rib joins the backbone). In the US, a rib roast is cut from the rib section; the equivalent English cut is from the *best end* section.
Rolled cutlets	See Scaloppine entry, below.
Scaloppine or veal scallops	Very thin *escalopes* or *fillets* Scaloppine are small, thin pieces of veal leg, pounded to $1/8$" to $1/16$" thick, and usually sautéed or braised. When they are rolled with a stuffing, tied and braised, they're known as veal birds or rolled cutlets; when they are deep-fried, they're wiener schnitzel.
Shank cross cut	This cut of meat is a cross cut from the foreshank section (called the *foreknuckle* section in England).
Shoulder blade roast	*Shoulder roasting joint with blade bone*

VEAL CUTS, *cont.*

	This roast is cut from the shoulder section and contains a portion of the blade bone. (The area it's cut from is called the *neck*, *middle neck*, and *shoulder* sections in England.)
Shoulder blade steak	These steaks (also known as shoulder veal chops or veal blade steak) are cut from the shoulder blade roast, and are less expensive than veal rib chops or loin chops.
Shoulder roast, boneless	*Shoulder roasting joint, boneless* This roast is cut from the shoulder section, has the bones removed, and is rolled and tied.
Shoulder steak, boneless	*Shoulder roasting joint, boneless, cut up into steaks* Boneless shoulder steaks are steaks cut from the boneless shoulder roast.
Sirloin steak, boneless	Boneless sirloin steak is cut from the loin section (in England, the section of loin adjoining the rump).
Top loin chops	Top loin chops are loin chops with tenderloin removed.

VEAL CUTS, *cont.*

Top round steak	This steak is cut from the top of the leg (the round section in the US; the *leg fillet* section in England).
Veal birds	See Scaloppine.
Veal patties	These are veal burgers and are made from ground (*minced*) neck, shoulder, breast, and/or leg meat.
Veal saddle	This section of the animal is comprised of the two loins and part of the rump section (in England, the *loin*, *rump*, and part of the *leg fillet* section).
Veal stew	Veal stew is made from pieces of boneless meat of varying sizes, usually cut from the shank and shoulder sections (in England, the *foreknuckle*, and *neck* and *shoulder* sections).
Wiener schnitzel	See Scaloppine.

MEASUREMENTS

The Measurements section consists of the following:

Remember that for many of the same words (e.g., pint; gallon), the American and British amounts are not equal, so be sure to look in the correct column. I've listed the British measurements in **boldface** and the metric measurements in *italic*.

In most sections of this book and in the tables that follow, the equivalent amounts listed have been rounded off. (For an exact equivalent, see the Dry Weights and Fluid Volumes Conversion Tables where I've listed the full figures for calculations.)

By the way, you'll notice that as the UK becomes more and more metric, our product sizes are working their way towards metric-oriented rather than pound-oriented amounts (e.g., 500g rather than 454g [1 lb.]), so keep an eye out for this when shopping.

DRY WEIGHTS (QUICK REFERENCE)

This 'at a glance' Dry Weights chart should help you find your metric equivalents quickly. The avoirdupois amounts are listed to the left of their metric equivalents. For weights over 40 ounces, see page 76 for the calculations.

Avdp.	Metric	Avdp.	Metric
1 oz.	28 g	21 oz.	595 g
2 oz.	57 g	22 oz.	624 g
3 oz.	85 g	23 oz.	652 g
4 oz.	113 g	(1½ lb.) 24 oz.	680 g
5 oz.	142 g	25 oz.	709 g
6 oz.	170 g	26 oz.	737 g
7 oz.	198 g	27 oz.	765 g
(½ lb.) 8 oz.	227 g	28 oz.	794 g
9 oz.	255 g	29 oz.	822 g
10 oz.	283 g	30 oz.	850 g
11 oz.	312 g	31 oz.	879 g
12 oz.	340 g	(2 lb.) 32 oz.	907 g
13 oz.	369 g	33 oz.	936 g
14 oz.	397 g	34 oz.	964 g
15 oz.	425 g	35 oz.	992 g
(1 lb.) 16 oz.	454 g	36 oz.	1020 g
17 oz.	482 g	37 oz.	1049 g
18 oz.	510 g	38 oz.	1077 g
19 oz.	539 g	39 oz.	1106 g
20 oz.	567 g	(2½ lb.) 40 oz.	1134 g

FLUID VOLUME (QUICK REFERENCE)

This 'at a glance' chart has separate columns for US and British fluid ounces so be sure to look in the right one (although the slight difference isn't really noticeable until you get up into gallons). For weights over 20 ounces, see page 75 for the calculations.

US	Metric	UK	Metric
1 fl. oz.	30 ml	1 fl. oz.	28 ml
2 fl. oz.	59 ml	2 fl. oz.	57 ml
3 fl. oz.	89 ml	3 fl. oz.	85 ml
4 fl. oz.	118 ml	4 fl. oz.	114 ml
5 fl. oz.	148 ml	5 fl. oz.	142 ml
6 fl. oz.	177 ml	6 fl. oz.	170 ml
7 fl. oz.	207 ml	7 fl. oz.	199 ml
8 fl. oz.	237 ml	8 fl. oz.	227 ml
9 fl. oz.	266 ml	9 fl. oz.	256 ml
10 fl. oz.	296 ml	10 fl. oz.	284 ml
11 fl. oz.	325 ml	11 fl. oz.	313 ml
12 fl. oz.	355 ml	12 fl. oz.	341 ml
13 fl. oz.	384 ml	13 fl. oz.	369 ml
14 fl. oz.	414 ml	14 fl. oz.	398 ml
15 fl. oz.	444 ml	15 fl. oz.	426 ml
16 fl. oz.	473 ml	16 fl. oz.	455 ml
17 fl. oz.	503 ml	17 fl. oz.	483 ml
18 fl. oz.	532 ml	18 fl. oz.	511 ml
19 fl. oz.	562 ml	19 fl. oz.	540 ml
20 fl. oz.	591 ml	20 fl. oz.	568 ml

MILK CHART (BRITISH)

% Fat	British milk
	⇦ Skimmed Milk: 0.1% avg. fat (max: 0.3%)
0.5	
1.0	
1.5	Semi-skimmed milk (sometimes ⇦ labelled *half-fat milk*): 1.6% avg. fat content (min: 1.5%; max: 1.8%)
2.0	
2.5	
3.0	
3.5	Whole Milk: 3.8-3.9% avg. fat (min: 3.5; max: 4.2%)
4.0	
4.5	Channel Islands Milk (sometimes labelled *Breakfast Milk*): 4.8-5.1% avg. fat
5.0	(min. 4% fat)

MILK CHART (AMERICAN)

% Fat	American milk
	Skim or Nonfat Milk: *less than* 0.5% fat
0.5	
1.0	⇦ 1% Milk Lowfat Milk: 0.5% to 2% fat
1.5	
2.0	⇦ 2% Milk
2.5	
3.0	
3.5	
4.0	Whole Milk: *at least* 3.5% fat (though this minimum may vary from state to state in the US)
4.5	
5.0	

CREAM CHART (BRITISH)

% Fat	British creams
10	⇦ Half cream: 12-13% avg. fat
	⇦ Half-fat crème fraîche: 15% avg. fat
20	⇦ Single cream & Soured cream: 19% avg. fat for single cream (min. 18% fat)
30	↕ Crème fraîche: 30-35% fat
40	⇦ Whipping cream: 39% avg. fat content (min. 35% fat)
50	⇦ Double cream: 48% fat
60	↑ Clotted cream: 55%-63.5% avg. fat

CREAM CHART (AMERICAN)

% Fat	American creams
10	Half & Half: 10.5 to 11.7% avg. fat (min: 10.5%; max: 18%)
20	⇦ Sour cream: *at least* 18% Light cream or coffee cream: 18% to 30%
30	Light whipping cream: 30-36% fat
40	Heavy whipping cream or heavy cream: 36-40%
50	
60	

EGG SIZES (EEC)

British egg sizes are based on a weight per egg. When an American recipe calls for an egg and doesn't specify a size, use an egg weighing about 2 ounces (a Medium egg based on the current EEC egg sizes).

Current EEC Egg Sizes (as of January, 1998)

Small	*under 53g*	under 1.87 oz.
Medium	*53-63g*	1.87-2.22 oz.
Large	*63-73g*	2.22-2.57 oz.
XL or Very Large	*73g and above*	2.57 oz. and above

Old EEC Egg Sizes (prior to January, 1998)

7	*under 45g*	~1.57 oz.
6	*45-50g*	~1.68 oz.
5	*50-55g*	~1.85 oz.
4	*55-60g*	~2 oz.
3	*60-65g*	~2.2 oz.
2	*65-70g*	~2.38 oz.
1	*70-75g*	~2.5 oz.
0	*over 75g*	~2.65 oz.

Current EEC egg weights courtesy the Ministry of Agriculture, Fisheries, and Food. Old EEC egg weights courtesy the British Egg Information Service.

EGG SIZES (AMERICAN)

American egg sizes are based on a minimum weight per dozen eggs, as set by the US Department of Agriculture. The individual egg weights below were calculated based on the weight per dozen.

American Egg Sizes

Small	*~43g*	1.5 oz.
Medium	*~50-57g*	1.75-2.0 oz.
Large	*~57-64g*	2.0-2.25 oz.
Extra large	*~64-71g*	2.25-2.5 oz.
Jumbo	*~71g*	2.5 oz.

The minimum weight per dozen eggs, as set by the US Department of Agriculture, is as follows:

Size	Minimum weight per dozen eggs
Small	at least 18 ounces
Medium	at least 21 ounces
Large	at least 24 ounces
Extra Large	at least 27 ounces
Jumbo	at least 30 ounces

FOOD MASS EQUIVALENTS

A cup is a measure of volume, not of weight, and the weight of a cupful of something can vary, sometimes significantly (as with courgettes). So use the table below as only a loose guide and, if what you are cooking seems too wet or too dry, adjust the other ingredients until its consistency seems right.

Food	Amount	Equivalent
Bananas, 3-4 medium	1¾ cups, mashed	1 lb. (*454g*)
Beans, dried (*see Legumes*)		
Beans, fresh green	3-3½ cups	1 lb. (*454g*)
Butter, 1 stick	½ cup (or 8 Tbl.)	4 oz. (*113g*)
Cabbage, shredded	3½-4 cups	1 lb. (*454g*)
Carrots, chopped or sliced	3 cups	1 lb. (*454g*)
Carrots, shredded	2½-3 cups	1 lb. (*454g*)
Celery, chopped or sliced	½ cup	1 medium stalk
Cheese, cottage	1 cup	½ lb. (*227g*)
Cheese, shredded	1 cup	¼ lb. (*113g*)
Cocoa	4 cups	1 lb. (*454g*)
Cornmeal	3 cups	1 lb. (*454g*)
Flour, all purpose (*plain*)	4 cups	1 lb. (*454g*)
Flour, wholewheat (*wholemeal*)	3¾-4 cups	1 lb. (*454g*)
Gelatin	1 envelope (or 1 Tbl.)	¼ oz. (*7g*)
Graham cracker crumbs	1 cup	15 crackers

FOOD MASS EQUIVALENTS, cont.

Food	Amount	Equivalent
Honey	1⅓ cups	1 lb. (*454g*)
Lard	2 cups	1 lb. (*454g*)
Legumes:		
Beans, kidney	2½ cups	1 lb. (*454g*)
Beans, navy	2 cups	1 lb. (*454g*)
Lentils	2¼ cups	1 lb. (*454g*)
Peas, split	2¼ cups	1 lb. (*454g*)
Marshmallows, 16 large, cut-up	1 cup	4 oz. (*113g*)
Marshmallows, 90 miniature	1 cup	2 oz. (*56g*)
Mushrooms, sliced	5-6 cups	1 lb. (*454g*)
Nuts	1 cup	5 oz. (*142g*)
Oatmeal (uncooked)	5¾ cups	1 lb. (*454g*)
Onions, chopped	2-2½ cups (or 4 medium onions)	1 lb. (*454g*)
Raisins, seedless	2¾ cups	1 lb. (*454g*)
Salt, kosher	¼ cup	1.1 oz. (*30g*)
Salt, regular table salt	¼ cup	2.2 oz. (*60g*)
Sugar, brown (packed)	2¼ cups	1 lb. (*454g*)
Sugar, confectioners (*Icing sugar*)	3½-4 cups	1 lb. (*454g*)
Sugar, granulated	2 cups	1 lb. (*454g*)
Wheatgerm	3 cups	12 oz. (*340g*)
Yeast, compressed	1 cake	1 pkg. active dried
Yeast, active dried	1 package (*appr. 5g*)	1 Tbl.

AMERICAN COOKING EQUIVALENTS

Keep in mind that when American recipes call for teaspoons and tablespoons, *level* spoonfuls are meant; when British recipes call for teaspoons and tablespoons, *rounded* or *heaping* spoonfuls are meant. Two American (level) tablespoons are roughly equal to one British (heaped) tablespoon.

US measure	**British measure**	US fl. oz.	*Metric*	other US measures
60 drops	**1 tsp.**			1 tsp.
teaspoon	**1 tsp.**		*5 ml*	$^1/_3$ Tbl.
	dessert-spoon*	$^1/_3$ oz.	*10 ml*	2 tsp.
Tablesp.	**$^1/_2$ oz.**	$^1/_2$ oz.	*15 ml*	3 tsp.
fluid oz.	**1 oz.**	1 oz.	*30 ml*	2 Tbl.
$^1/_4$ cup	**2 oz.**	2 oz.	*59 ml*	4 Tbl. *or* $^1/_2$ gill
$^1/_3$ cup	**coffee cup**	$2^2/_3$ oz.	*79 ml*	$5^1/_3$ Tbl.
$^1/_2$ cup	**$^1/_5$ pint**	4 oz.	*118 ml*	8 Tbl. *or* 1 gill
1 gill	**4 oz.**	4 oz.	*118 ml*	$^1/_2$ cup *or* 8 Tbl.
$^2/_3$ cup	**teacup; 1 gill****	$5^1/_3$ oz.	*158 ml*	
$^3/_4$ cup	**$6^1/_4$ oz.**	6 oz.	*177 ml*	12 Tbl.

* The US has no dessertspoon measure.
** In Britain, the gill is 5 oz. ($^1/_4$ Brit. pint) but in the north and west of England it is 10 oz. ($^1/_2$ Brit. pint).

AMERICAN COOKING EQUIVALENTS, cont.

US measure	**British measure**	US fl. oz.	*Metric*	other US measures
1 cup*	**breakfast cup**	8 oz.	*237 ml*	1/2 pint *or* 2 gills *or* 16 Tbl.
1 pt.	**4/5 pint**	16 oz.	*473 ml*	2 C *or* 1/2 qt.
1 qt.	**33 1/3 oz.**	32 oz.	*946 ml*	4 C *or* 2 pts. *or* 1/4 gal.
1/2 gal.	**66 2/3 oz.**	64 oz.	*1.89 l*	4 pts. *or* 2 qts.
1 gal.	**133 oz.**	128 oz.	*3.78 l*	8 pts. *or* 4 qts.

Note: tsp. = teaspoon; Tbl. or T. = tablespoon; C = cup; pt. = pint; qt. = quart; and gal. = gallon.
Also, *ml = millilitre* and *l = litre.*

AMERICAN CAN SIZES

Can size	Equivalent Weights
No. 300	14-16 ounces *(395-455g)*
No. 303	16-17 ounces *(455-480g)*
No. 2	1 lb., 4 oz. (i.e., 20 oz.) *(565g)* *or* 1 US pt., 2 fl. oz. (i.e., 18 oz.) *(530ml)*
No. 2½	1 lb., 13 oz. (i.e., 29 oz.) *(820g)*
No. 3	46 ounces *(1.3kg)*

* The British standard cup is 10 ounces but ordinary cups are more commonly used in British kitchens.

FLUID VOLUMES AND FLUID VOLUME CONVERSION TABLES

A fluid ounce is a measure of *volume* rather than weight so the actual weight of a fluid ounce will vary according to the density of what is being weighed. The volume, however, will not vary and litres, centilitres, and millilitres are measures of volume.

1 US ounce = *29.57 millilitres*
1 US pint = 16 US ounces
1 US quart = 2 US pints = 32 US ounces
1 US gallon = 4 quarts = 8 US pints = 128 US ounces

1 British ounce = *28.41 millilitres*
1 British pint = 20 British ounces
1 Imperial gallon = 8 British pints = 160 British oz.

1 litre = 100 centilitres = 1,000 millilitres

TO CONVERT FROM METRIC:

From:	To:	Multiply by:
Millilitres	US fl. oz.	0.03381497
Millilitres	US pint	0.002113436
Millilitres	**British fl. oz.**	0.03519609
Millilitres	**British pint**	0.001759804
Centilitres	US fl. oz.	0.3381497
Centilitres	US pint	0.02113436
Centilitres	**British fl. oz.**	0.3519609
Centilitres	**British pint**	0.01759804
Litres	US fl. oz.	33.81497
Litres	US gallon	0.2641794
Litres	**British fl. oz.**	35.19609
Litres	**Imperial gallon**	0.2199755

FLUID VOLUME
CONVERSION TABLE, cont.

TO CONVERT FROM AMERICAN:

From:	To:	Multiply by:
fl. ounce (US)	**British fl. ounce**	1.040843
fl. ounce (US)	*millilitres*	29.57
fl. ounce (US)	*litres*	0.029572702
pint (US)	**British pint**	1.2009638
pint (US)	*millilitres*	473.12
pint (US)	*litres*	.47312
gallon (US)	**Imperial gallon**	0.83267
gallon (US)	*litres*	3.785306

TO CONVERT FROM BRITISH (IMPERIAL):

From:	To:	Multiply by:
fl. ounce (Brit.)	US fl. ounce	0.9607594
fl. ounce (Brit.)	*millilitres*	28.41
fl. ounce (Brit.)	*litres*	0.02841225
pint (British)	US pint	.8326645
pint (British)	*millilitres*	568.2
pint (British)	*litres*	.5682
gallon (Imperial)	US gallon	1.20095
gallon (Imperial)	*litres*	4.546

DRY WEIGHTS AND DRY WEIGHT CONVERSION TABLE

With the exception of large commercial weights and the fact that the American system has no stone,[*] dry weights are the same for the US and the UK, so 1 US lb. (avoirdupois) = 1 British lb. (avoirdupois).

1 ounce = *28.35 grams or 2835 milligrams*
1 pound (16 ounces) = *454 grams or .454 kilograms*
1 kilogram = 1,000 grams or 1,000,000 milligrams

TO CONVERT TO METRIC:

From:	To:	Multiply by:
ounces	*grams*	28.349523
ounces	*kilograms*	0.0283
pounds	*grams*	453.59237
pounds	*kilograms*	0.45359237

TO CONVERT FROM METRIC:

From:	To:	Multiply by:
grams	ounces	0.035273962
kilograms	pounds	2.2046

---

[*] A stone equals 14 pounds.

*LINEAR MEASURE**

1 inch = *2.54 centimetres*
1 foot = *30.48 centimetres*
1 yard = *91.44 centimetres or .9 metre*

1 centimetre = 0.39 inch
1 metre = 39.37 inches

1 millimetre = .1 centimetre
1 centimetre = 10 millimetres
1 metre = 100 centimetres or 1,000 millimetres
1 kilometre = 1,000 metres

TO CONVERT TO METRIC:

From:	To:	Multiply by:
inches	*centimetres*	2.54
feet	*centimetres*	30.4801
yards	*metres*	0.914
miles	*kilometres*	1.609

TO CONVERT FROM METRIC:

From:	To:	Multiply by:
centimetres	inches	0.39370079
centimetres	feet	0.0328
metres	yards	1.094

---

* There is no difference between British and American inches, feet and yards.

TEMPERATURES

OVEN TEMPERATURES

Fahr.	*Cels.*[*]	Gas Mark	Descriptions
225	*110*	¼	
250	*120*	½	very slow
275	*135*	1	
300	*150*	2	slow
325	*160*	3	moderately slow
350	*175*	4	moderate
375	*190*	5	moderately hot
400	*205*	6	hot
425	*220*	7	
450	*230*	8	very hot
475	*245*	9	
500	*260*	10	extremely hot[**]

---

[*] The Celsius temperatures listed in this chart are approximate equivalents to their corresponding Fahrenheit temperatures.

[**] This is the temperature bakers use to bake bread rolls; it is too hot for home baking.

TEMPERATURES, continued

AIR TEMPERATURES

Fahr.	Cels.	Fahr.	Cels.
32	0	149	65
41	5	158	70
50	10	167	75
59	15	176	80
68	20	185	85
77	25	194	90
86	30	203	95
95	35	212	100
104	40	221	105
113	45	230	110
122	50	239	115
131	55	248	120
140	60	257	125

To convert from Fahrenheit to *Celsius*:
  Subtract 32; and then divide by 1.8.

To convert from *Celsius* to Fahrenheit:
  Multiply by 1.8; and then add 32.

ADDRESSES

The following is a very brief list of shops that carry American foods and cooking ingredients. For further addresses, check the current edition of the *Food Lovers' Guide to Britain*, published by BBC Books.

Alma Delicatessen
    89 Lower Precinct, Coventry CV1 1DS
    Tel: 01203-228898

Essington Fruit Farm *(for picking your own fruit)*
    Bognop Rd., Essington, Wolverhampton WV11 2BA
    Tel: 01902-735724 (ring first to be sure the fruit you want is ready for picking)

Fortnum & Mason
    181 Piccadilly, London W1A 1ER
    Tel: 0171-734-8040

Harrods Ltd.
    Knightsbridge, London SW1X 7XL
    Tel: 0171-730-1234
    Fax: 0171-581-0470

Note: *Jerry's Homestore specialise in furnishings but as they do carry some American foods, I've included their addresses.*

Jerry's Homestore
    163 Fulham Road, London SW3
    Tel: 0171-581-0909 Fax: 0171-584-3749
    57 Heath Street, Hampstead, NW3
    Tel: 0171-794-8622 Fax: 0171-794-8427
    concessions in 4th floor Harvey Nichols, Knightsbridge SW1
    Tel: 0171-245-6251 Fax: 245-1179

Jerry's Homestore branches, *cont.*
   The Bentall Ctr., Kingston upon Thames, Surrey
   Tel: 0181-549-5393 Fax: 0181-549-9106

Lupe Pintos (*primarily Mexican-American foods*)
   24 Leven Street, Edinburgh
   Tel: 0131-228-6241
   Fax: 0131-228-2390

Note: *Made in America are a mail-order business that specialise in American foods, including difficult-to-find items such as masa harina.*
Made in America -- The American Store
   Unit 5B, Hathaway Retail Park, Chippenham,
   Wiltshire SN15 1JG
   Tel: 01249-447558
   Fax: 01249-446142

Partridges of Sloane Street
   132/134 Sloane Street, London SW1
   Tel: 0171-730-0651 & 0171-730-7102/3
   Fax: 0171-730-7104

Panzer Delicatessen
   13-19 Circus Road, St John's Wood, London
   NW8 6PB
   Tel: 0171-722-8596

Susman's Best Beef Biltong Co. (*Beef jerky & biltong by mail order*)
   36 Hillcrest Rd., E. Sussex BN9 9EG
   Tel: 01273-516160

James Trehane & Sons (*for blueberry picking*)
   Stapehill Road, Hampreston, Wimborne, Dorset
   BH21 7ND
   Tel: 01202-873490 (ring first to be sure fruit is
   ready for picking)

Note: *Trustins are a supplier of international foods. To find the shop nearest you that carries a particular American product supplied by Trustin, write Trustin, enclosing a self-addressed, stamped envelope, and tell them what you're looking for.*

Trustin the Foodfinders
   Chase Rd., Northern Way, Bury St Edmunds,
   Suffolk IP32 6NT
   Tel: 01284-766265

R. Walsh & Co. Ltd. (*Walsh's manufacture an extract for making sarsaparilla beer; they're not a shop*)
   121 Rear Hamilton St., Blackburn, Lancashire

INDEX

HOW TO ORDER ADDITIONAL COPIES

You may order additional copies of this pocketbook; the main book; or both together (at a saving).

To order:
- write to the address below, stating the number of copies required, and of which book(s);
- enclose a cheque made out to *Glencoe House Publications* to cover the total cost of the copies, and their postage and packaging.

To order the main book:	To order the pocketbook:	To order both books:	
American Cooking in England	*The Pocketbook Guide to American Cooking in England*		£17.99
		p&p:	2.75
		total:	**£20.74**

main book:	£14.99	pocket-book:	£3.99
p&p:	2.75	p&p:	.30
total:	**£17.74**	total:	**£4.29**

Send your order and cheque to:
Glencoe House Publications
189 Anglesey Road
Burton upon Trent
Staffordshire
DE14 3NS